We See the Cloud

Poems by Moira Butterfield, June Crebbin and Celia Warren

Illustrations by Jenny Wren

Collins

Contents

How to Predict the Weather　3
Wind Force!　4
Frost　6
Cold　7
Seasons　8
Umbrellas　10
Walking on Leaves　12
Puffins　14
Song of the Emperor Penguins　16
DECEMBER England　18
DECEMBER Australia　19
We See!　20
Viewpoints　21
Flood　22
Sandstorm　24
Rainforest　26
And Now Here is the Weather for Astronauts …　28
What is the weather doing today?　30

How to Predict the Weather

Grandma said:
"If you see a bright red sky at night,
The weather next day will be all right.
Look out for a red sky in the morning.
It's usually a heavy rain shower warning.
Oh, and if cows sit down, it's a sign of rain.
You'll find I'm right, in the main."

I said:
"OK, I'll watch for skies and cows.
But do you mind if, just for now,
I stay indoors and watch TV?
There's a weather forecast on, you see!"

Moira Butterfield

Wind Force!

Wind force zero: calm, no chill,
the gentle sea lies smooth and still.

Wind force one: ripples run,
smoke drifts as if for fun.

Wind force two: a light breeze,
leaves rustle in the trees.

Wind force three: the breeze is soft,
lightweight flags are held aloft.

Wind force four: a moderate breeze,
small branches quiver in the trees.

Wind force five: the wind is fresh,
white caps on the sea as the waves thresh.

Wind force six: the wind is stirring,
overhead wires are whistling and whirring.

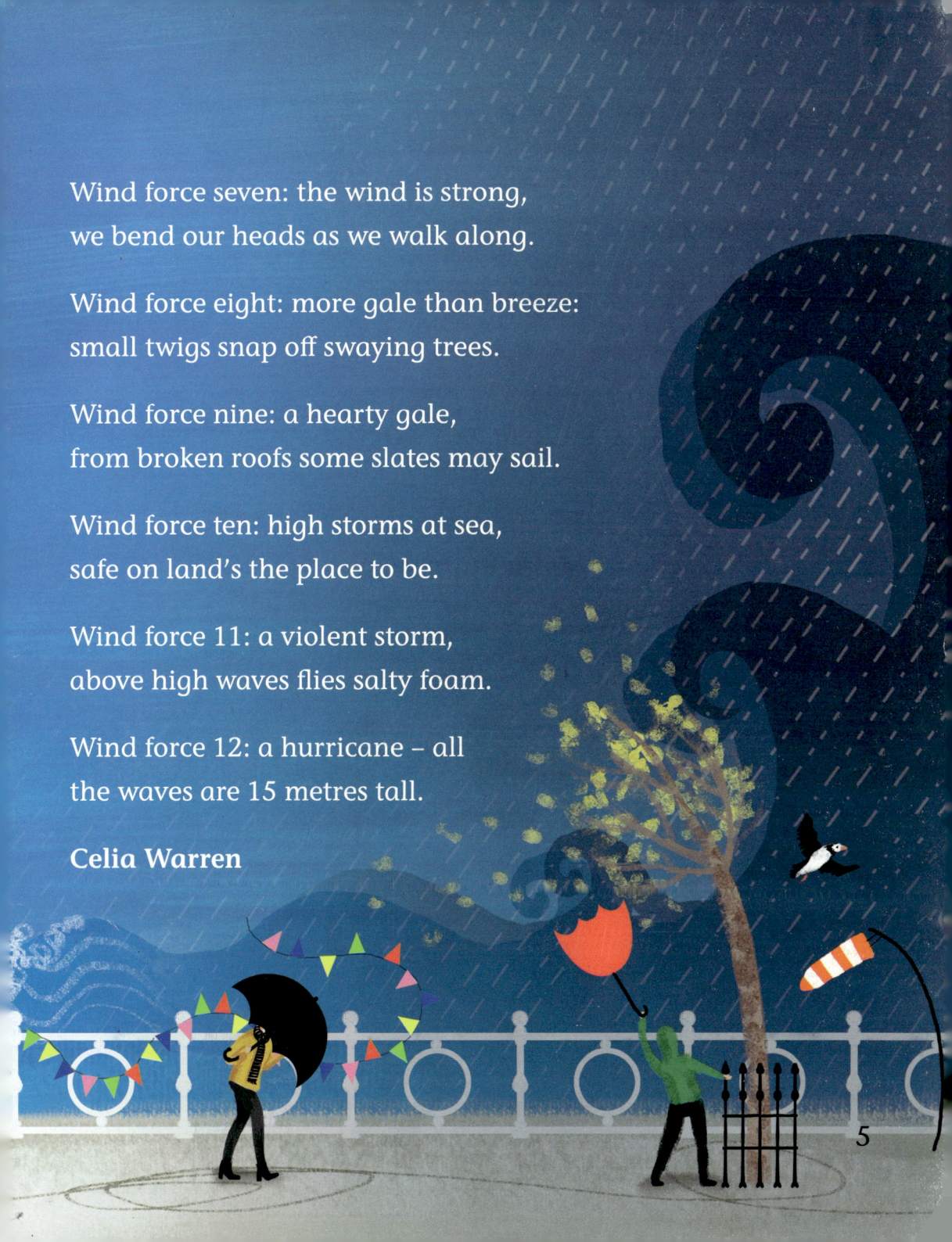

Wind force seven: the wind is strong,
we bend our heads as we walk along.

Wind force eight: more gale than breeze:
small twigs snap off swaying trees.

Wind force nine: a hearty gale,
from broken roofs some slates may sail.

Wind force ten: high storms at sea,
safe on land's the place to be.

Wind force 11: a violent storm,
above high waves flies salty foam.

Wind force 12: a hurricane – all
the waves are 15 metres tall.

Celia Warren

Frost

Frost sneaks silently.
It weaves its white carpet
without even a whisper.

But if you touch it,
you can unlock its secret
CRUNCH!

Moira Butterfield

Cold

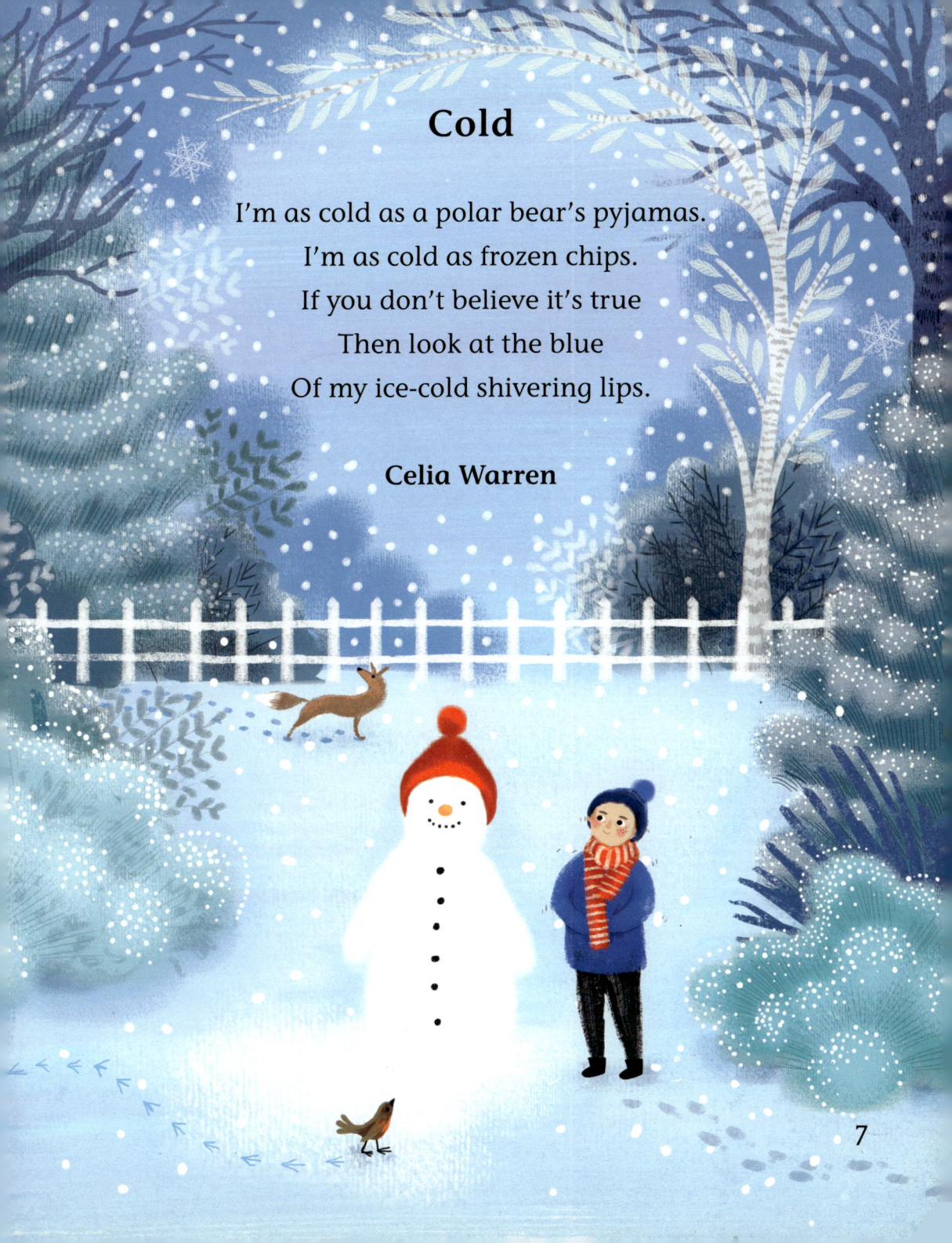

I'm as cold as a polar bear's pyjamas.
I'm as cold as frozen chips.
If you don't believe it's true
Then look at the blue
Of my ice-cold shivering lips.

Celia Warren

Seasons

Sunny
December day:
leaves locked inside creaking
puddles; frozen where they fell from
the trees.

March wind
whistles and whines.
Warm scarves tied tightly.
Daffodils' golden trumpets blow
laughter.

Cloudless
blue August sky
filled with birds, butterflies
and the soft drone of humming bees.
Dogs sleep.

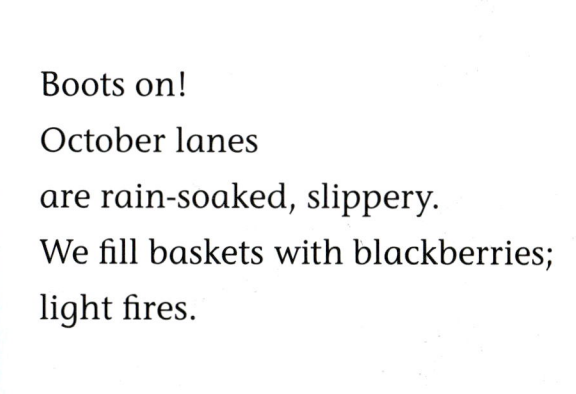

Boots on!
October lanes
are rain-soaked, slippery.
We fill baskets with blackberries;
light fires.

Celia Warren

Umbrellas

I lost umbrella number one.
I left it on a train.
It was blue with lots and lots of spots,
and perfect for the rain.

I got umbrella number two
another rainy day.
It was quite a price and very nice
but I lost it anyway.

Umbrella number three was great.
I think it was the best …
… the brightest green I've ever seen,
I lost it like the rest.

I'm giving up umbrellas.
I don't care if it pours.
The next time it starts to rain,
I'm going back indoors.

Moira Butterfield

Walking on Leaves

Leaves of gold and crimson
Curl crisply on the street,
Their papery voices chatter
As they crunch beneath my feet.
It's early Monday morning
And the sun is warm and sweet.

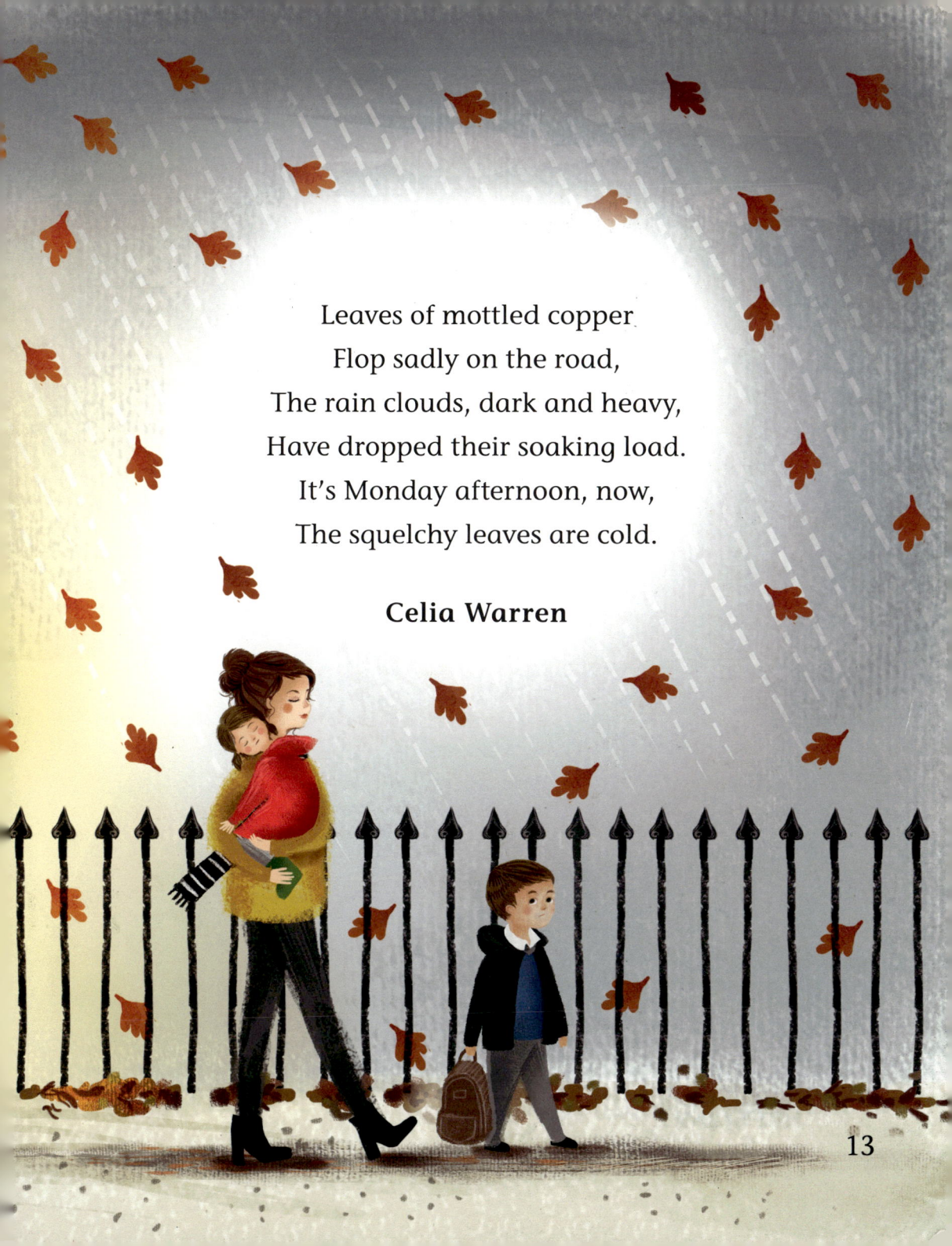

Leaves of mottled copper
Flop sadly on the road,
The rain clouds, dark and heavy,
Have dropped their soaking load.
It's Monday afternoon, now,
The squelchy leaves are cold.

Celia Warren

Puffins

We are going to see the puffins,
but the mist has come down,
covering the cliff face.

We can hear the puffins calling;
we can hear their wings
whirring like helicopter blades.

We can see the notice which says:
"PUFFINS CAN BE SEEN FROM HERE",
but we cannot see the puffins.

Mist seeps into our faces,
our noses, our eyes,
it hangs in the air –

Wait, it is beginning to drift,
to roll away in folds
under a pale sun.

Puffins! Hundreds of puffins!
The cliff face is alive with puffins,
feeding, landing, flying.

June Crebbin

Song of the Emperor Penguins

Down in Antarctica,
where snow and ice belong,
see the Emperor penguins,
listen to their song:

"Let's do the huddle-cuddle,
let's keep warm,
let's snuggle up together,
free from harm.

Let's do the scuffle-shuffle,
through deep snow,
let's change places,
in and out we go.

Let's do the waddle-poddle,
let's keep our heat,
let's keep our eggs warm
on our feet."

Down in Antarctica,
all winter long,
see the Emperor penguins,
listen to their song.

June Crebbin

DECEMBER
England

When icicles hang by the wall,
and the pond is frozen over,
when swirling snowflakes round us fall
and sheep by the hedge take cover,
we slide on sledges again and again,
hoping perhaps there'll be
time for a snowball fight and then …
… toasted crumpets for tea!

June Crebbin

DECEMBER
Australia

When the sun is high in the sky,
and surfers ride the waves,
when everyone's spirits are high,
in these lazy, summer days,
we build sand castles with turrets and towers,
dig channels that reach to the sea,
go fishing in rock pools for hours,
… then, barbecued burgers for tea!

June Crebbin

We See!

I see a snail.
Fred sees a whale.
I see a frog.
Fred sees a dog.
I see a cat.
Fred sees a bat.

We're both looking at ...
... a cloud!

Moira Butterfield

Viewpoints

Wind whips the sea
into blue soup and cream:
a sailor's nightmare,
a painter's dream.

Celia Warren

Flood

Every year, when the rains come,
the big river floods,
spreading its waters over the fields,
helping the rice to grow.

But, if the rain is too heavy,
the waters rise too high,
rice fields are washed away,
roads disappear.

Then, boats are needed,
to rescue people from their houses,
carry animals to safety,
– and take us to school!

June Crebbin

Sandstorm

Once,
along this shore,
blew a wind so fierce,
it whipped the sand into a storm
and buried a village.

For 5,000 years
the village lay hidden,
no one knew,
until …

one day,
along this same shore,
blew a wind so fierce,
it stripped the sand away,

revealing a village,
with stone houses, jewellery,
tools made of wood and bone,
still there,
which you can see today.

June Crebbin

Rainforest

With a parrot's screech
and a monkey's howl,
in heat that bakes
the forest wakes.
Its leaves are cupped;
a water trap,
like thirsty hands
beneath a tap.
But rain can't cool
a tree-frog's pool
when the forest drinks.

A calm canopy
hides the ants
that tickle and tease
the tallest trees.
Vibrant flowers
thrive below
with all that creep
and sleep and grow.
In the humid heat
to its own heartbeat
the forest sinks.

Celia Warren

And Now Here is the Weather for Astronauts ...

Today on Mars it will be cold,
chilly enough to freeze you solid.

On Venus a wild wind will blow,
strong enough to smash your teeth.

On Saturn lightning bolts will hit,
hot enough to fry you up.

On Jupiter stinking clouds will swirl,
bad enough to block your breath.

On Earth the sun will shine all day,
so put your space rocket away!

Moira Butterfield

29

What is the weather doing today?

frosty

snowy

rainy

sunny

windy

misty

Ideas for reading

Written by Gillian Howell
Reading and literary resources consultant

Learning objectives: read aloud books closely matched to improving phonic knowledge, sounding out unfamiliar words accurately, automatically and without undue hesitation; reread these books to build up fluency and confidence in word reading; recognising simple recurring literary language in stories and poetry; discussing favourite words and phrases; continuing to build up a repertoire of poems learnt by heart, appreciating these and reciting some, with appropriate intonation to make the meaning clear

Curriculum links: Science, Art, Geography

Interest words: weather, ripples, rustle, lightweight, moderate, whistling, whirring, pyjamas, mottled, Emperor penguins, Antarctica, icicles, fierce, vibrant, astronauts

Word Count: 1,107

Resources: poetry anthologies, paint and paper

Getting started

This book can be read over two or more reading sessions.

- Look together at the front cover and read the title. Ask the children what they think the book might be about.
- Turn to the back and read the blurb to the children using an expressive tone. Ask the children again what sort of book this will be.
- Turn to p2 and ask them to read the list of contents. Establish that this book is a collection of poems with the theme of weather

Reading and responding

- Ask the children to look through the book and read four or five poems of their choice.
- Encourage them to identify poetic features as they read, e.g. rhyme, rhythm, alliteration, simile and metaphor, and interesting uses of vocabulary.